Thérèse of Lisieux

On the visit of her relics
to Great Britain

*All booklets are published thanks to the
generous support of the members of the
Catholic Truth Society*

CATHOLIC TRUTH SOCIETY
PUBLISHERS TO THE HOLY SEE

Contents

Foreword 3

Being involved 5

Who was St Thérèse? 7

Her Little Way of Spiritual Childhood 13

St Thérèse and Prayer 17

Her Family Life and Vocation 21

Patroness of the Missions 25

Why do we venerate relics? 27

The Little Way of St Thérèse in her own words 37

Prayers for use before and during the visit 51

Where and how to venerate the relics 63

Itinerary of the visit 65

Further information 69

Foreword

I am delighted to introduce this booklet which has been produced to help all who will be taking part in the visit of the Relics of St Thérèse to England and Wales.

Following requests from a number of quarters, and with the agreement of my fellow bishops, I was very happy to write to the Rector of the Shrine of St Thérèse in Lisieux in December 2007, requesting that our country join the 40 or so others around the world which have received her Relics in pilgrimage. A positive reply was not long in coming, and preparations for the visit began.

Why have the bishops made this invitation? One obvious answer is that St Thérèse is greatly loved in this country. One has only to look at the number of parish churches dedicated to her, the number of statues and pictures of her to be found in people's homes as well as in public places, and the books that have been written about her and her message by British authors to see this. So the visit of her Relics will be an opportunity to deepen our communion with God through devotion to her, and to ask her intercession for our needs.

St Thérèse is a saint for everybody, not just for Catholics. Many Christians of other Churches are strongly drawn to her; and her message, which is simply the Gospel of Christ for our times, has the power to help those of any faith or none. It is my prayer and hope that the visit of her Relics will be a great blessing to many people in England and Wales and to our entire country.

✠ Cardinal Cormac Murphy-O'Connor

Being Involved

The purpose of this booklet is to help you prepare for the visit of St Thérèse's Relics to England and Wales, and to get the most out of it. At the end of the booklet you will find practical information about where and how to venerate the Relics. The rest of the booklet explains why St Thérèse is so important to us today and why Catholics venerate relics. It also offers suggestion for prayer and reflection based on St Thérèse's own writings.

St Thérèse spent most of her life in Lisieux, a town in Normandy, Northern France, and it is there that her mortal remains are kept. Since 1994 the custom has grown up of taking portions of her Relics around France and the whole world in pilgrimage, and it is from Lisieux that they will be travelling to us.

The Relics, consisting of portions of her leg and thigh bones, are contained in a large, sealed casket. Upon arrival in England, they will be taken around in a roughly clockwise direction for about a month, staying in churches and cathedrals for between one and three days. The venues have been chosen to enable as many people as possible in England and Wales to visit them without having to travel too far.

To prepare for the visit, many places are organising talks or other events which will be advertised locally. You can also use this booklet to read about St Thérèse's importance as a spiritual teacher, and you will find many suggestions for further reading here and on the website, *www.catholicrelics.co.uk*.

Prayer is a very important part of preparing for the visit. Ask God to show you what you should pray for, both for yourself and for others, when you come to venerate the Relics. Pray that it will bring many graces to all who come, and to our whole land.

Who was St Thérèse?

Born in Alençon, France on 2nd January, 1873, Thérèse was the youngest of nine children, four of whom died in childhood. Her father Louis was a watchmaker and her mother Zélie ran a small lace-making business. The Martin family was a very happy one and her childhood was in many ways idyllic. Sadly tragedy struck when her mother developed breast cancer and died on 28th August, 1877. After her death the family moved to Lisieux.

Thérèse took to heart the deep spirituality she experienced in her home. From an early age prayer and friendship with God were very important to her. Her father was exceptionally loving and affectionate. She saw these as qualities of God, her Heavenly Father.

There was however another side to her life. Her mother's death had quite a traumatic effect. Thérèse asked her sister Pauline to be mother to her. When Pauline became a Carmelite nun it was if she had lost a second mother. The two losses led to several bouts of illness which seemed to result more from her emotional state than any physical cause. She tells of a remarkable conversion of spirit on Christmas Eve 1884, which healed her childhood immaturity and led to a very strong calling to become a Carmelite nun.

St Thérèse of Lisieux.

Thérèse considered that she was stubborn but this often expressed itself in great determination, particularly in the way she followed her call. When the prioress of the Carmelites refused to allow her to enter because she was so young, the formerly shy girl spoke to the local bishop. She describes how she put her hair up to make herself look older. However the bishop was not willing to let her enter so she decided to go to the Pope.

Some months later her father took Thérèse and Céline, her sister, on a visit to Rome. In the course of an audience with Pope Leo XIII she begged him to let her enter. While the Pope's reply that, "If it is God's will, you will enter" initially saddened her, she gradually become aware of its importance. She wanted to do God's will at all costs. Thérèse's determination and spirit of prayer on that trip made an impression on the Bishop's Vicar-General. On 9th April, 1888 Thérèse was admitted to the Carmelite convent and took the name St Thérèse of the Child Jesus and the Holy Face.

Thérèse embraced her new life with enthusiasm and generosity. Convent life was not easy. The accommodation was very basic and there was little heat to counter the bitterly cold winters. Not all of the community warmed to her. In her *Story of a Soul* she mentions several incidents that cost her dearly. One sister in the community took a dislike to her and took every opportunity to let her know that. Thérèse's response was to react in love - to the point that the sister once asked her why Thérèse liked her so much!

Thérèse had a great love of Scripture. She was especially fond of the Gospels and carried a small book of the Gospels near her heart at all times. There she came to know Jesus and discovered what she describes as her "Little Way" of spiritual childhood - a way of confidence and trust and of total surrender to God's merciful love. In St Paul's second letter to the Corinthians Thérèse found her vocation: to be love at the heart of the Church.

Thérèse loved nature. As a child she remembered a visit to the beach at Deauville and the sense of wonder that the waves created in her. She loved flowers. It is not surprising that she uses flowers to describe the kingdom of God. She sees herself as one of the little flowers and hence is often referred to as "The Little Flower".

Suffering was a constant part of Thérèse's life. For her it was a way of imitating Jesus in his love for his Father and for all of humanity. One of the greatest traumas in Thérèse's life was her father's illness. A series of strokes led to hallucinations and he had to live in a mental institution. She also had several periods of inner darkness in her life and a particularly intense period in the eighteen months before she died. During the last period she found it hard to believe in any spiritual reality. In the latter part of her life she also suffered from poor health and developed tuberculosis. She died on 30th September, 1897 at the age of twenty four.

Her dream was to spend her heaven doing good on earth, to let fall from heaven a shower of roses. Since her death many people have attributed to the intercession of St Thérèse graces they have received, problems that have been resolved, healings that have taken place. The presence or scent of roses is often associated with healings or other blessings. St Thérèse has kept her promise to let fall a shower of roses.

Thérèse was beatified in 1923 and canonised in 1925. Within three years of her canonisation she was declared Patroness of the Missions. St Thérèse had never been a missionary though she had offered to go to the Carmel at Hanoi. She had however dedicated her life to pray for missionaries. Thérèse also offered her suffering for the missions. There is a very touching incident towards the end of her life when one of the sisters suggested that it might be better for her to walk less as it was taking such a toll on her. Her response was, "It is true, it is an effort, but do you know what gives me strength? I offer every step for some missionary, thinking that somewhere far away, one of them is worn out from his labours and, to lessen his fatigue, I offer mine to God."

She wrote an account of her life, which she described as the *The Story of a Soul*. Published shortly after she died it has proved remarkably popular with people of many different cultures and faith traditions and has been translated into over fifty languages. In recognition of the influence of her writings on the development of spirituality in the twentieth century Pope John Paul II declared her a Doctor of the Church in 1997.

Her *Little Way* of Spiritual Childhood

The *Little Way* is St Thérèse's trademark, the core and centrepiece of her spirituality. It was not something she invented; she discovered it in the gospels. It was God's special gift to her and, through her, to the Church of our day. With such a fresh and revolutionary doctrine she opened a new window on the gospel and made holiness accessible in a way most of us had never thought possible.

Thérèse always wanted to be a great saint but was all too conscious of her poverty and her weakness: 'When I compare myself to the saints it is like the difference between a mountain that soars into the clouds and an obscure grain of sand.' But she refused to be discouraged; 'God,' she reminded herself, 'cannot inspire unreasonable desires.' So she looked for another way, 'a way that is direct, very short and totally new.' This we now call the *Little Way* - the way of spiritual childhood - or, as Thérèse herself preferred to call it, 'the way of littleness'.

The heart of a child

For her, the first step was to recognise her weakness and her frailty, to learn to live with her own brokenness and her constant need for God's mercy. For a long time she tried to 'make it on her own', to earn God's love and merit heaven by her own efforts. Thérèse grew up in an age when the prevailing spiritual atmosphere relied almost exclusively on merit and achievement. The law of sacrifice predominated; heaven was approached by backing away from hell. Thérèse was taught to keep an account with God; she even had a special notebook to record all her virtues, good deeds and self-sacrifices!

Gradually a deeper reality emerged; the law of love replaced the law of merit. Her littleness, she realised, was not a hindrance to the fulfilment of her desires but the very foundation on which it was built and the reason for her confidence. 'Jesus does not teach me to count my acts of virtue,' she wrote. 'He teaches me to do all through love.' Love is at the very heart of the *Little Way*. 'Our Lord has shown me the only way that leads to love - it is the way of childlike trust and self-surrender, the way of a child that sleeps, afraid of nothing, safe in its mother's arms.' The *Little Way* means doing by grace what a child does by nature.

The people's saint

Thérèse has been called 'the universal saint' and rightly so. In the same way, Dorothy Day referred to her as 'the people's saint', an extraordinary claim about someone whose life was hidden, cloistered and unknown. But the truth is that it was she who brought holiness out of the cloister and into the streets, into the home and into the workplace. Behind the veil, the grille and the cloister, people recognised one of themselves, someone who sanctified the ordinary, the humdrum and the everyday. She is the democrat of holiness. Long before the Second Vatican Council sounded the call for universal holiness, Thérèse already issued that same call to her 'legion of little souls'. She saw clearly that holiness is not the private province of monks in the desert or nuns in the cloister. It is the gift of the Father's love to all who seek it with the heart of a child.

And what is more, Thérèse succeeds where Councils so often fail. She not only spoke of the universal call to holiness, she shows us *how* to achieve it. She has the ability to touch the heart and inspire a dream more directly and more powerfully than any document. A doctrinal statement is one thing; the living witness of a saint is another.

The greatness of the Little Way

The greatness of her *Little Way* is that it is not great but very ordinary. To love is the most natural thing in the world. God's love is equally accessible; we do not have to earn it or win it. It is a gift; all we have to do is to accept it, as Thérèse did, with empty hands. God does not love us because of what we do or what we are; he loves us because of who he is and what he is. If he did not love us, he would cease to be God! 'Jesus has no need of our works, but only of our love.' This is the way of spiritual childhood, the way of confidence and trust. The path to love *is* love: 'It is confidence and nothing but confidence that will lead us to love.'

The universal call to holiness is a call to love. It is the *Little Way* in action. They are one and the same thing: the gospel, in a word. This is the heart of Thérèse's message, a message proclaimed so clearly that even a child can understand. God is love and we, despite all our brokenness and our frailty - yes, even our sinfulness -, are called not only to receive it but also to live it and even celebrate it. It is the love-song of the Gospel.

St Thérèse and Prayer

You will hardly ever find people, either saints or sinners, content with the way they pray. One can say prayers, but there are so many distractions; it all seems so complicated; God seems at times not to hear. Is there some book, some method or some technique that would lead us to "real" prayer, which seems an impossible ideal?

An official teacher

Thérèse has a very simple idea of prayer:

"For me, prayer is a surge of the heart; it is a simple look turned towards heaven, it is a cry of recognition and love, embracing both trial and joy."

This little sentence from her *Story of a Soul* is more than a pious idea of a poorly educated saint. It has become official teaching of the Church since it was placed at the very beginning of the fourth part of *The Catechism of the Catholic Church* devoted to prayer (n. 2558). We can say that all that the *Catechism* has to say on prayer (307 articles over 67 pages) is therefore to be seen as a commentary on the simple statement of Thérèse. Her teaching covers all kinds of prayer - set vocal prayer, the Eucharist, the Rosary, and meditative, reflective or contemplative prayer.

A surge of the heart

Prayer is not primarily what we say. Indeed the *Catechism* introduces the text of Thérèse by saying that prayer is about "a vital and personal relationship with the living and true God." As such it is a matter of the heart, of our inmost being, of our whole person. As a surge of the heart, prayer reflects our present actual experience. A surge of the heart is not a carefully composed statement. It is coming to God as we are, speaking with complete honesty.

A simple look towards heaven

Any prayer is a statement of our insufficiency, of our need. The source of our strength is not our own power. Like the psalmist, we "lift up our eyes to the mountain" (*Ps* 121:1). The look is directed to the One who loves, whom we have learned to trust. Prayer for Thérèse is not a big speech or explanation to God. She simply looks towards God.

A cry of recognition and love

Prayer is between Thérèse and God: they recognise one another. She can be confident that as she turns to God, God has already turned to her. That is enough. Prayer is only an expression of a trusting relationship. We recall that the last words Thérèse was able to write in her life story were "confidence and love". These sum up her life and are the foundation of her prayer.

Embracing both trial and joy

The more we learn about Thérèse the greater is our appreciation of her heroic love. At one level she seems to have had a simple and trouble free life at home and in the Lisieux Carmel. In reality, she had continual problems of sickness, relationships and even a struggle to hold on to her faith when God seemed to withdraw from her in the final two years of her life. But she is telling us that whether we feel joyful or in distress, our response should be to stretch out our whole being to God.

Difficulties in prayer

Thérèse's life seen in her autobiography, *The Story of a Soul*, as well as her letters and other writings show that she encountered every problem in prayer that we ourselves might meet. Her sister Céline stated that Thérèse suffered dryness in prayer practically all her life. You might not guess this reading her poetry, which she wrote to encourage others, mostly her sisters in the Carmel. She might seem to have an immediate experience of divine things, but in reality she was only expressing what dry faith taught her rather than what she felt.

She had a lifelong difficulty with the Rosary, which pained her deeply. She loved Our Lady very much, but this prayer was almost torture to her. She kept saying it. She knew that what Mary her Mother wanted was her love, not nice thoughts or sentiments.

She knew all about distractions, but did not worry: what mattered was that God loved her, and she loved God.

She found praying with others difficult. Her response was to offer up the prayers of her companions to God in place of her own poorer efforts.

When the well of prayer seemed to be completely dry, her last resort was to say the *Our Father* or the *Hail Mary* very slowly. Such praying soothed her soul and brought peace.

Simple but not easy

St Thérèse manifested grit all her life, or as St Teresa of Avila said, "a determined determination." She kept going. For her prayer was not fits and starts; it was a daily cultivation of a love relationship with the God who was drawing her into intimacy.

Her Family Life and Vocation

"In the heart of the Church my mother I will be love." These remarkable words expressed with joy by St Thérèse at the age of twenty-two reveal a depth of faithfulness to grace from the dawn of her consciousness. She was born towards the latter part of nineteenth-century France, the ninth and last child of devout and loving parents. A lively, intelligent and very affectionate child she was deeply loved and cherished by her parents and sisters, and any temptation to pamper her was balanced by the need for moral training within a Christian context.

Hers was a family, indeed, who quite simply and unashamedly referred everything to God - joys and sorrows, hopes and struggles were lived in a spirit of deep faith and regular participation in the life of the Church. The young Thérèse thrived in such a loving atmosphere. She writes "all my life God was pleased to surround me with love and my earliest memories are stamped with smiles and the most tender caresses," and again "having such good example around me, I naturally wanted to follow it." Perhaps without this experience of being so held and loved, her vocation might have been stifled.

However, her love for her parents was so deep that she developed an unusually precocious sensitivity to their wishes, shedding copious tears if she was naughty. After one such incident her mother recounts "pardon was quickly granted, I pressed my little one to my heart and covered her with kisses." This tender reciprocal love with her parents was to develop into a profound yet simple theology of spiritual childhood.

Role of suffering

Suffering too played its part in the story of her vocation. The premature death of her mother when she was only four years old and the subsequent entry of her two older sisters to Carmel were devastating blows for her fragile psyche and she eventually collapsed under the strain. Her lively and spontaneous character disappeared and she became diffident and withdrawn, finding comfort only within her immediate family and through the attention of her devoted father, whose goodness and prayerfulness helped her discern her own vocation: "One only had to look at him praying to know how to pray."

During these years of inner turmoil and clinging, Thérèse, supported by her family, maintained her deep vision of faith, fuelled by her very helplessness, which drew her ever closer to her Lord. This was crucial; a very real work was taking place in her soul, creating an opening for grace, and leading her rapidly towards

Carmel. It was on Christmas Eve, 1886, when an offhand remark from her tired father triggered a remarkable transformation of character: "The work I had been unable to do in ten years was done by Jesus in one instant, contenting Himself with my goodwill which was never lacking." She felt the need to forget herself and work entirely for the conversion of others. A vocation was born.

In a remarkably short space of time this young girl had wasted no experience - suffering, weakness, faith and joys all became vehicles through which she saw ever more clearly the hand of her Lord. She was ready to take a leap forward in the mysterious adventure of faith: Carmel beckoned.

St Thérèse of Lisieux.

Patroness of the Missions

How did St Thérèse, an enclosed Carmelite nun, whose only journey outside France was to Rome to petition the Pope, become Patroness of the Missions?

The reason is simple: because contemplative community life revolves around prayer for the entire world and the needs of the entire people of God. St Thérèse was just such a nun - simply faithful to her vocation.

Thérèse knew of world events within the limitations of technology and her Carmelite life. Her letters to missionaries offered the hope and encouragement essential for building and sustaining an infant Church. She said, *'A Carmelite who would not be an apostle would draw away from the goal of her vocation... Since I could not be an active missionary, I wanted to be one through love and penance.'*

The vocation of Thérèse was that of an all-embracing love, extending beyond Carmel, encompassing those parts of the world new to the Gospel message.

Unable to do 'big things', she believed her 'little way' would bring herself and others to Jesus. *'I have come (to Carmel) to save souls. Jesus let me understand that it was through the cross that he wanted to give me souls. It is through prayer and sacrifice that we can help the missionaries.'*

Thérèse's commitment to Mission led Pope Pius XI to declare her Patroness of the Missions on 14th December 1927. Her feast is particularly celebrated in areas under the care of the Congregation for the Evangelisation of Peoples.

'I would like to travel over the earth... I would like to proclaim the Gospel even in the most remote islands. I would go to those who have never heard about the Lord: I would proclaim his glory to the nations and offer them as a present to my God.'

Why do we Venerate Relics?

One of the distinctive marks of Catholic Christianity is the honour it pays to the saints - those Christian men and women who, over the centuries, have been generally recognized as being striking examples of holiness: as people, that is, who truly and often at great cost make the love of Christ present in the world through his Church. We do not just honour the saints, however (as we might honour the memory of a great leader or artist), as people whose example is worth following; we also ask for their intercession - for their prayers. We do this because they, like us, are members of the Church, the Body of Christ, which is a mystical reality of mutual love and support. This is the "Communion of Saints" we profess belief in when we say the Creed. Asking the saints in heaven to pray for us is exactly like asking other Christians we know in this life to pray for us; except that, unlike us, the saints' love and knowledge of God have been purified and fulfilled by their loving embrace of the cross God chose for them. Just as their life in Christ is now, after earthly death, incomparably fuller than ours, so their prayers, we may reasonably think, are more likely to be heard. The history of Christianity is filled with stories of extraordinary help received after the intercession of saints has been asked. Stories of favours received after praying to St Thérèse are particularly numerous and striking.

Relics of Saints

This, most people would admit, is clear enough. But what about relics of the saints? The central liturgical document of the Second Vatican Council, the constitution *Sacrosanctum Concilium*, says, "Traditionally, the saints are honoured in the Church and their genuine relics and images are held in veneration" (§111).[1] Why does the Church invite us to honour the physical remains of these Christians of the past?

Relics are usually divided into three sorts, or classes. The most important, known as "first class" relics, are parts of the actual bodies of the saints; next are "second class" relics, which are things owned or used by the saint when alive; lastly, "third class" relics have been touched to the body or tomb of the saint after his or her death.

How can we begin to understand this, though? First of all, we need to remember that we human beings are not primarily spirits, with a body as a tool or appendage or something we are only short-term tenants of; primarily, we *are* our bodies, and Christianity is fundamentally a religion of the body, founded on the fact of the Incarnation: of God's being born in a body like ours.

By virtue of the Incarnation, because Jesus Christ was a human being with a physical body like ours, the human body is now a fundamentally holy thing, with potential and capacity to be transformed and transfigured as his was first on Mount Tabor, and then at Easter. We are called, through the cross, to a death like his, and also like him to resurrection into glory.

So, if people are holy, they are also holy in their bodies; the dogma of the Virgin Mary's Assumption makes it clear that, for all Christians, both body and soul are wholly redeemed and live only in the hope of a fuller life. St Paul says that our earthly bodies will be transformed into "glorious" bodies (*Ph* 3:21) like Christ's; at the resurrection, we will "reassume the likeness of the heavenly Adam" (1 *Co* 15:49). Birth to new life through death is not merely a "spiritual" truth (which could easily become just a metaphorical or symbolic statement) but also a profoundly physical one. Exactly what this will mean is not certain; but incidents in the lives of the saints (such as the "transfiguration" experienced by the orthodox St Seraphim of Sarov) make the profoundly physical, and transforming, nature of holiness very clear.

So, if our bodies are potentially holy, or in the case of the saints actually so, then it seems reasonable to honour what remains of them after physical death. These remains, or relics, are both a sign or token of the glory to come, and (just as the bread and wine at Mass are transformed into the Body and Blood of Christ) will in some mysterious way be physically continuous with their glorified future.

There is a useful reminder here, too; if the Communion of Saints is purely spiritual, then what we do with our bodies now doesn't matter (this is exactly the misunderstanding St Paul wrote to the Corinthians to correct[2]); but if holiness is bodily too, then how we live in our physical selves is as important as what we think or believe.

Other relics

What about second and third class relics? Well, it is or should be obvious that we can and do affect the world around us: what we do, and arguably even what we say, produces a real change in the physical realities, the things that make up the world in which we live (which is also, we should remember, God's world, and the things in it, God's creatures). If this ability to change the world, then, (which some have called "subcreative") is a basic human gift, then surely any physical thing intimately associated with another person is in some way changed in its nature. Most people have an intuitive grasp of this. When we say that a particular thing has "sentimental value", we are not necessarily indulging in sentimentality in the sense of wishful thinking. If, then, this is true of all human beings, how much more so is it true of those who are outstanding in holiness. The Church's history is crammed full of stories about particular favours God has chosen to grant through the medium of a physical object that has been associated with a holy person: a relic, in fact.[3] Now, this may bring us back again to the business of bones: if the things a person has used may be somehow imprinted and changed by this, and in some way known to God can act as a means of grace, how much more so can the physical remains of their very selves, their bodies.

Perhaps this seems too abstract, or "mystical", or wrapped in the language of theology. Maybe it is more helpful to think how we want to touch the people we admire. Venerating of relics allows us to do this; and it is not morbid or peculiar if, as Christians, we firmly believe that the saints are not dead, but live now in Christ a life that is truly real.

In light of all this, perhaps we can understand why, from the earliest times, the Church has always encouraged Christians to venerate relics.[4] In the early Church, the Eucharist was often celebrated above the tombs of martyrs; to this day, a church cannot be consecrated without at least one relic placed in the altar.

St Thérèse's Relics

Normally people travel on pilgrimage to where a holy person is venerated. In the case of Thérèse we can see that in a sense she is coming to us. Beginning in 1994, and particularly after 1997 when she was named a Doctor of the Church, Thérèse's relics - which are major bones - have been taken to visit dozens of countries across the world.

We can connect these travels of St Thérèse's relics with something she once wrote: "I have the vocation of an apostle. I would like to travel over the whole earth to preach your name and to plant your glorious cross on infidel soil. But oh, my beloved, one mission would not be enough for me, I would want to preach the Gospel on all five continents simultaneously and even to the most remote isles. I would be a missionary, not for a few years but from the beginning of creation until the consummation of the ages." Obviously, during her life she lived as an enclosed nun; but God does not break his promises, and since her death she has been all round the world and even into space.

Thérèse's relics have visited numerous sites in France, and also Belgium, Germany, Italy, Austria, Switzerland, the Netherlands, Slovenia, Bosnia-Herzogovina, Spain, Ireland, and Malta; and, outside Europe, Brazil, Argentina, Mexico, Canada, the United States, Russia, Kazakhstan, Siberia, Australia, Polynesia, the Philippines, Taiwan and Hong Kong, Madagascar, the Seychelles, Egypt, the Lebanon, Benin, and Iraq. In all these places a visit of the relics of Thérèse has been welcomed as a great grace, and been attended with great devotion and many testimonies of spiritual and physical favours received, adding to the thousands of such testimonies that began almost as soon as her story became known. We should remember the promise Thérèse made just before she died: "I intend to spend my heaven doing good on earth. After my death, I shall make a shower of roses rain down."

In June 2008, one of the astronauts on the space shuttle Discovery carried a relic of St Thérèse into space, where, for fourteen days, she circled the earth whilst the Carmelite nuns in Texas who had provided the relics commended the whole world to her care. In 1927 Pope Pius XI named her as universal patron of missions. We may see her visit to England as just another step in her continuing apostolate.

In England and Wales, the Little Way Association assists the missionary work of the Catholic Church across the world.

With faith in God's loving mercy, we trust that St Thérèse's prayers will bring about great things in our country as they already have across the world.

Favours received

Thousands of testimonies to the favours received through the prayers of St Thérèse of Lisieux have been collated and published worldwide and there is every reason to hope that people who pray before the Relics during their visit to England and Wales will receive similar blessings.

Sally

The Relics' visit to America during late 1999 and early 2000 created huge media interest, but aside from that and more importantly, lives were powerfully touched and changed. Sally Davies visited the Relics at a Carmelite Monastery after she had recently married. One of the Carmelite sisters later wrote: "Sally came to ask for prayer because she had discovered that she had a tumour and she was very anxious about it. She explained that she had never been to a Carmel before... The sister that she spoke to told her to place all her trust in God and that she should be assured of all the prayers of the Carmelite sisters." This same sister invited her to attend Mass during the forthcoming visit of the Relics to the Carmel.

On the day of the Relics' visit, the testimony continues: "A Carmelite sister was helping two small altar servers approach the Relics when she saw Sally place her hand on the casket and she prayed that Thérèse would take pity on her... Two weeks later, a radiant Sally knocked at the Carmel door. She had been to see her doctor and the tumour had disappeared... She told the sister that after the Mass on the day of the Relics' visit, when she returned to her car, her mother asked what perfume she was wearing. Sally responded that she wasn't wearing any that day, but she too smelt the odour of roses."

Daire

Daire was a sceptic and visited the Relics in a church in Ireland in the year 2000. She wrote: "Grotesque, macabre, horrifying, even sickening. When I heard about the visit of St Thérèse and her bones, and read the hype about the imminent 'tour', I couldn't believe what I was hearing. Why would anyone in their right mind go see a dead nun's bones from the nineteenth century? But, despite my protestations, the curiosity still got the better of me. The Relics of St Thérèse were visiting my hometown. People were touching the casket, praying to it; some were even weeping, overcome by it all. Me? I was just thinking how many bones you could fit in that space, and why did it have to be in a glass case?"

"For me it wasn't the presence of the Relics that struck me, but the pervading atmosphere of serenity… we all just sat there, in complete silence… I sat there with my thoughts and just pondered… For me it wasn't really about the bones or the legacy. It became a small moment that brought me back into the fold of the Church and community."

Iraq

In 2002 the Relics headed for the troubled country of Iraq. The blessings of the visit were many, not least, renewed hope and the many positive effects on young people. The Archbishop of Bagdad, Most Rev Jean Sleiman said that St Thérèse helped "those who had lost hope to rediscover hope." He added: "The thing that most struck me about the crowds who were praying to Thérèse in Iraq, was the percentage of young people there. Available for the preparatory work, numerous celebrations, desiring always to know more, the youth generally gave the impression that they had been seduced by this 'young woman contemplative'... She showed them how their uncertainties and sufferings can be transfigured through love."

The Little Way Association is based in London and assists the missionary work of the Catholic Church across the world, providing chapels, homes, schools and a wide variety of help to the needy overseas. Thérèse is its patron and the team testify to receiving two or three letters a month from benefactors giving thanks to the saint for favours received through her prayers. We await with expectant faith that St Thérèse's prayers will bring about great things in our land as she already has across the world.

The Little Way of St Thérèse in her own Words

I am a very little soul, who can offer only very little things to the Lord.

Vocation

I feel in me the vocation of the priest. With what love, O Jesus, I would take you in my hands when, at my voice, you would come down from heaven. And with what love would I give you to souls! But alas! While desiring to be a priest, I admire and envy the humility of St Francis of Assisi and I feel the vocation of imitating him in refusing the sublime dignity of the Priesthood.

Jesus, my Love, my vocation, at last I have found it…my vocation is love! Yes, I have found my place in the Church and it is You, O my God, who have given me this place; in the heart of the Church, my Mother, I shall be love.

Universal love

I see now that true charity consists in bearing with the faults of those about us, never being surprised at their weaknesses, but edified at the least sign of virtue… Should the devil draw my attention to the faults of one of them… I call to mind at once her virtues and her good intentions.

Love proves itself by deeds, so how am I to show my love? Great deeds are forbidden me. The only way I can prove my love is by scattering flowers and these flowers are every little sacrifice, every glance and word, and the doing of the least actions for love.

God's grace and our good works

In the evening of this brief day, I shall appear before you with empty hands, for I do not ask you, Lord, to count my works. In your eyes all our justice is blemished. Therefore will I robe myself in your own justice and receive from your love the eternal possession of yourself.

Everything is a grace, everything is the direct effect of our Father's love - difficulties, contradictions, humiliations, all the soul's miseries, her burdens, her needs - everything, because through them, she learns humility, realises her weakness. Everything is a grace because everything is God's gift. Whatever be the character of life or its unexpected events - to the heart that loves, all is well.

Childlike trust in God

One can never have too much confidence in the good God. I shall love him to the point of recklessness. I will never put limits to my confidence.

Sometimes, when I read spiritual treatises, in which perfection is shown with a thousand obstacles in the way and a host of illusions round about it, my poor little mind soon grows weary, I close the learned book, which leaves my head splitting and my heart parched, and I take the Holy Scriptures. Then all seems luminous, a single word opens up infinite horizons to my soul, perfection seems easy; I see that it is enough to realise one's nothingness, and give oneself wholly, like a child, into the arms of the good God. Leaving to great souls, great minds, the fine books I cannot understand, I rejoice to be little because 'only children, and those who are like them, will be admitted to the heavenly banquet'.

Self-surrender

Jesus deigns to point out to me the only way which leads to Love's divine furnace, and that way is self-surrender: it is the confidence of the little child who sleeps without fear in its father's arms. Through the mouth of Solomon, the Holy Spirit has said: 'Whosoever is a little one, let him come unto me,' and elsewhere the same Spirit of Love declares that 'to him that is little, mercy is granted' (*Ws* 6:6). In his name, too, the Prophet Isaiah reveals how on the last day the Lord 'shall feed his flock like a shepherd: he shall gather together the lambs with his arm, and shall take them up into his bosom' (*Is* 40:11).

And, as though all these proofs were insufficient, the same Prophet, whose inspired gaze penetrated the depths of eternity, cried out: 'Thus saith the Lord: You shall be carried at the breasts and upon the knees they shall caress you. As one whom the mother caresseth, so will I comfort you' (*Is* 66:12, 23).

If all weak and imperfect souls such as mine felt as I do, none would despair of reaching the summit of the mountain of Love, since Jesus does not look for deeds, but only for gratitude and self-surrender.

Now I have no further desire unless it be to love Jesus even unto folly! Love alone draws me. I wish for neither suffering nor death, yet both are precious to me, and I have long called upon them as the messengers of joy. Already I have suffered much; already it has seemed to me that my barque was nearing the Eternal Shore. From my earliest years I believed the Little Flower would be gathered in her springtime, but now the spirit of self-abandonment is my sole guide - I have no other compass. I am no longer able to ask eagerly for anything save the perfect accomplishment of God's design on my soul.

I desire neither death nor life. Were Our Lord to offer me my choice, I would not choose. I only will what he wills, and I am pleased with whatever he does. I have no fear of the last struggle, or of any pain, however great, which my illness may bring. God has always been my help; he has led me by the hand since I was a child and I count on him now. Even though suffering should reach its furthest limits I am certain he will never forsake me.

Keeping little

How little known is the merciful love of the Heart of Jesus! It is true that to enjoy that treasure we must humble ourselves, must confess our nothingness...and here is where many a soul draws back.

It is possible to remain little even in the most responsible position, and besides is it not written that at the last day 'The Lord will arise and save the meek and lowly ones of the earth'? (cf *Ps* 75:10) He does not say 'to judge' but 'to save'!

You do wrong to find fault, and to try to make everyone see things from your point of view. We desire to be as little children. Now, little children do not know what is best. Everything is right in their eyes. Let us imitate them.

When we keep little we recognise our own nothingness and expect everything from the goodness of God, exactly as a little child expects everything from its father. Nothing worries us, not even the amassing of spiritual riches.

Again, being as a little child with God means that we do not attribute to ourselves the virtues we may possess, in the belief that we are capable of something. It implies, on the contrary, our recognition of the fact that God places the treasure of virtue in the hand of his little child for him to use as he needs it, though all the while it is God's treasure.

Finally, to keep little means not to lose courage at the sight of our faults. Little children often tumble, but they are too small to suffer grievous injury.

Courage

Do not let your weakness make you unhappy. When, in the morning, we feel no courage or strength for the practice of virtue, it is really a grace: it is the time to 'lay the axe to the root of the trees', (*Mt* 3:10) relying upon Jesus alone. If we fall, an act of love will set all right, and Jesus smiles. He helps us without seeming to do so; and the tears which sinners cause him to shed are wiped away by our feeble love. Love can do all things. The most impossible tasks seem to it easy and sweet. You know well that Our Lord does not look so much at the greatness of our actions, or even at their difficulty, as at the love with which we do them. What, then, have we to fear?

Patience with ourselves

It may be that at some future day my present state will appear to me full of defects, but nothing now surprises me. Nor does my utter helplessness distress me; I even glory in it, and expect each day to reveal some fresh imperfection. Indeed these lights on my own nothingness do me more good than lights on matters of faith.

The remembrance of my faults humbles me, and helps me never to rely upon my own strength, which is mere weakness. More than all, it speaks to me of mercy and of love. When a soul with childlike trust casts her faults into Love's all-devouring furnace, how can they escape being utterly consumed?

I know that many saints have passed their lives in the practice of amazing penance for the sake of expiating their sins. But what of that? 'In my Father's house there are many mansions' (*Jn* 14:2). These are the words of Jesus, and therefore I follow the path he marks out for me; I try to be nowise concerned about myself, and to abandon unreservedly to him the work he deigns to accomplish in my soul.

He reaches out his hand to us, the very moment he sees us fully convinced of our nothingness, and hears us cry out: 'My foot stumbles, Lord, but thy mercy is my strength' (*Ps* 93:18). Should we attempt great things, however, even under pretext of zeal, he deserts us. So all we have to do is to humble ourselves, to bear with meekness our imperfections. Herein lies - for us - true holiness.

Do not think we can find love without suffering, for our nature remains and must be taken into account; but suffering puts great treasures within our reach. Indeed it is our very livelihood and so precious that Jesus came down upon earth on purpose to possess it. Of course, we should like to suffer generously and nobly; we should like never to fall. What an illusion! What does it matter if I fall at every moment! In that way I realise my weakness, and the gain is considerable. My God, thou seest how little I am good for, away from thy divine arms; and if thou leavest me alone, well, it is because it pleases thee to see me lie on the ground. Then why should I be troubled?

If you are willing to bear in peace the trial of not being pleased with yourself, you will be offering the Divine Master a home in your heart. It is true that you will suffer, because you will be like a stranger to your own house; but do not be afraid - the poorer you are, the more Jesus will love you. I know that he is better pleased to see you stumbling in the night upon a stony road, than walking in the full light of day upon a path carpeted with flowers, because these flowers might delay your advance.

Prayer of a little one

For me, prayer is an uplifting of the heart, a glance towards Heaven, a cry of gratitude and of love in times of sorrow as well as of joy. It is something noble, something supernatural, which expands the soul and unites it to God.

To secure a hearing there is no need to recite set prayers composed for the occasion… I have not the courage to search through books for beautiful prayers; they are so numerous, that it would only make my head ache, and besides, each one is more lovely than the other. Unable either to say them all or to choose between them, I do as a child would do who cannot read - I say just what I want to say to God, quite simply and he never fails to understand.

Giving pleasure to Jesus

When my state of spiritual aridity is such that not a single good thought will come, I repeat very slowly, the 'Our Father' and the 'Hail Mary', which suffice to console me, and provide divine food for my soul.

When I am in this state of spiritual dryness, unable to pray, or to practise virtue, I look for little opportunities, for the smallest trifles, to give pleasure to Jesus: a smile or a kind word, for instance, when I would wish to be silent, or to show that I am bored. If no such occasion offer, I try at least to say over and over again that I love him. This is not heard, and it keeps alive the fire in my heart. Even should the fire of love seem dead, I would still throw my tiny straws on the ashes, and I am confident it would light up again.

It is true I am not always faithful, but I never lose courage. I leave myself in the arms of Our Lord. He teaches me 'to draw profit from everything, from the good and from the bad which he finds in me' (St John of the Cross). He teaches me to speculate in the bank of love, or rather it is he who speculates for me, without telling me how he does it - that is his affair, not mine. I have but to surrender myself wholly to him, to do so without reserve, without even the satisfaction of knowing what it is all bringing to me... For I am not the prodigal child, and Jesus need not trouble about a feast for me - I am always with him.

Drawn by love

The days would be too short to ask in detail for the needs of each soul and I am afraid I might forget something important. Complicated methods are not for simple souls and, as I am one of these, Our Lord himself has inspired me with a very simple way of fulfilling my obligations.

One day, after Holy Communion, he made me understand these words of Solomon: 'Draw me: we will run after thee to the odour of thy ointments' (*Sg* 1:3). O my Jesus, there is no need then to say: In drawing me, draw also the souls that I love. The words 'Draw me' suffice. When a soul has been captivated by the odour of thy perfumes she cannot run alone; as a natural consequence of her attraction towards thee, all those whom she loves are drawn in her train.

In asking to be drawn, we seek an intimate union with the object that has led our heart captive. If iron and fire were endowed with reason, and the iron could say, 'Draw me!' would this not prove its wish to be identified with the fire to the point of sharing its substance? Well, such is precisely my prayer. I ask Jesus to draw me into the fire of his Love, and to unite me so closely to himself that he may live and act in me. I feel that the more the fire of love consumes my heart, the more frequently shall I cry, 'Draw me!' and the more also will those souls who come in contact with me run swiftly in the sweet odour of the Beloved.

The practice of love

Far from resembling those heroic souls who from their childhood use fast and scourge and chain to discipline the flesh, I made my mortifications consist simply in checking my self-will, keeping back an impatient answer, rendering a small service in a quiet way, and a hundred other similar things.

I have a longing for those heart-wounds, those pin-pricks which inflict so much pain. I know of no ecstasy to which I do not prefer sacrifice. There I find happiness, and there alone. The slender reed has no fear of being broken, for it is planted beside the waters of Love. When, therefore, it bends before the gale, it gathers strength in the refreshing stream, and longs for yet another storm to pass and sway its head. My very weakness makes me strong. No harm can come to me, since in whatever happens I see only the tender hand of Jesus... Besides, no suffering is too big a price to pay for the glorious palm.

I endeavoured above all to practise little hidden acts of virtue, such as folding the mantles which the Sisters had forgotten and being on the altar to render them help. I had also a great attraction towards penance, although I was not allowed to satisfy the desire. Indeed the only mortification I was permitted was the overcoming of my self-love, which did me far more good than any bodily penance could have done.

God does not despise these hidden struggles with ourselves, so much richer in merit because they are unseen: 'The patient man is better than the valiant, and he that ruleth his spirit than he that taketh cities.' Through our little acts of charity, practised in the dark, as it were, we obtain the conversion of the heathen, help the missionaries, and gain for them plentiful alms, thus building both spiritual and material dwellings for our Eucharistic God.

Hidden sacrifices

On another occasion when I was engaged in the laundry, the Sister opposite to me, who was washing handkerchiefs, kept splashing me continually with dirty water. My first impulse was to draw back and wipe my face in order to show that I wanted her to be more careful. The next moment, however, I saw the folly of refusing treasures thus generously offered, and I carefully refrained from betraying any annoyance. On the contrary I made such efforts to welcome the shower of dirty water that at the end of half an hour I had taken quite a fancy to the novel kind of aspersion, and resolved to return as often as possible to the place where such precious treasures were freely bestowed.

Offering little joys

It seems to me that if our sacrifices take Jesus captive, our joys make him prisoner too. All that is needed to attain this is that, instead of giving ourselves over to selfish happiness, we offer to our Spouse the little joys he scatters in our path to charm our hearts and draw them towards him.

Jesus enters your heart

Remember that our sweet Jesus is there in the Tabernacle expressly for you and you alone. Remember that he burns with the desire to enter your heart. Do not listen to the enemy. Laugh him to scorn, and go without fear to receive Jesus, the God of peace and of love...

I assure you I have found that this is the only means of ridding oneself of the devil. When he sees he is losing his time, he leaves us in peace.

In truth, it is impossible that a heart which can find rest only in contemplation of the Tabernacle - and yours is such, you tell me - could so far offend Our Lord as not to be able to receive him... What does offend Jesus, what wounds him to the heart, is want of confidence.

Heaven

I will spend my Heaven doing good on earth.
After my death I will let fall a shower of roses.

Eternal Peace.

Prayers for use before and during the visit

National Prayer for the Visit to England and Wales

God our Father, you reveal to us the depth of your love
in the holy face of Jesus Christ your Son.
As we honour St Thérèse of the Child Jesus
may we have the confidence and love
to stand fully in the light of your presence
so that the beauty of the Gospel may expand our hearts
and open us to the gifts of your Holy Spirit.

We make this prayer through Christ Our Lord.

Our Lady of Walsingham, pray for us.
St Thérèse, Patroness of the Missions, pray for us.

A Little Litany in Honour of St Thérèse of Lisieux

Teach us, Little Flower, to love as you did love in life the God of Love
Teach us, we pray, through the Holy Name of Jesus.
Show us the path to God through Mary's tender heart
Pray take our hand and be our guide
Teach us, Little Flower, to walk our way with childlike faith in God's good promise

Teach us, we pray, through the Holy Name of Jesus.

Show us in times of doubt the certainty of God's abiding love

Pray take our hand and be our guide

Teach us, Little Flower, to accept God's holy will for us with gentle patience

Teach us, we pray, through the Holy Name of Jesus.

Show us the way to trust and self-surrender

Pray take our hand and be our guide

Teach us, Little Flower, the beauty of holy innocence in this our time

Teach us, we pray, through the Holy Name of Jesus.

Show us the way to pray in love for this our world

Pray take our hand and be our guide

Teach us, Little Flower, to bear with joy and hope our trials and pain

Teach us, we pray, through the Holy Name of Jesus.

Show us the way of doing good on earth that we may also do good in heaven

Pray take our hand and be our guide

Teach us, Little Flower, to refuse nothing to God

Teach us, we pray, through the Holy Name of Jesus.

Show us the way, the truth and the light

Pray take our hand and be our guide

Saint Thérèse of the Child Jesus, pray for us
And all we are and all we are to be
That through your holy intercession and heroic virtues
We may each attain to that heavenly garden of roses,
The paradise of God's true promise.
In humble duty do we offer this litany of praise
To the glory of our loving Father
Who with Jesus, the Lamb of our redemption
And the Spirit our constant strength
Reigns one God in that same most blest garden
With all his angels and saints
Now and for everlasting, Amen.

Prayers for use during a Novena

Lord, Father of Mercy, St Thérèse relied on you for everything, just as a little child is dependent on her father. Her unconditional trust and childlike abandon gave her reason to hope "that you would do her will in heaven because she had always done your will on earth." I implore you to answer the prayer I address to you with faith and hope entrusting myself to her intercession, through Christ our Lord.

Our Father...

Lord Jesus, you are the only Son of God. You came into this world to give your life for sinners. St Thérèse responded to your call like a beloved spouse, passionate for your glory, living her life on earth out of love for you and for the salvation of souls, and she desired to "spend her heaven doing good on earth." Through her intercession, I place myself in your hands, imploring you to answer the prayer I address to you in complete confidence and trust.

10 Hail Mary's

Sweet Holy Spirit, Consoler and Father of the poor, you are the Lord, the giver of life, you are the source of all love. You inspired St Thérèse to desire holiness and to offer herself to merciful love, seeking nothing above the will of God. Through her intercession, I ask you to inspire my desires and requests, and to teach me how to pray in the inner sanctuary of my heart, where you dwell.

Glory be...

St Thérèse of the Child Jesus and the Holy Face, see the trust I have in you. Welcome my intentions and present them to the Most Holy Trinity. Unite me in a fraternal way to all those who ask your prayers.

Teach me patience and perseverance. Teach me how to offer all my trials, and to walk in trust and self-abandonment.

I particularly ask you to teach me to love, you who had "no greater desire than to love to the point of dying of love." Amen.

Prayer to the Little Flower
(From the Novena to Saint Thérèse)

O Saint Thérèse of the Child Jesus, who during thy short life on earth became a mirror of angelic purity, of love strong as death, and of whole-hearted abandonment to God, now that thou rejoicest in the reward of thy virtues cast a glance of pity on me as I leave all things in thy hands. Make my troubles thine own - speak a word for me to Our Lady Immaculate, whose flower of special love thou wert - to that Queen of Heaven 'who smiled on thee at the dawn of life'. Beg her as Queen of the Heart of Jesus to obtain for me by her powerful intercession the grace I yearn for so ardently at this moment, and that she join with it a blessing that may strengthen me during life, defend me at the hour of death, and lead me straight on to a happy eternity. Amen.

Petition

Lord Jesus, through the life of St Thérèse, you have brought new hope to all who long to open their hearts to you. Teach us the secret of her 'Little Way' and help us to realise that we can always talk with you and bring you our gratitude, our smiles and our tears.

Stay with us, Jesus, so that in the midst of our busy hours, we may turn to you in loving trust. Transform each passing moment of time into a moment of prayer. Fill every troubled heart with the confident faith of St Thérèse. In joy and in sorrow, in every circumstance, may our hearts rest in your peace. Amen.

Prayer to St Thérèse of the Child Jesus

Teach us how to open our hearts without reserve to the Holy Spirit as you did, to seek and find God's will in all the crises and choices, in the joys and disappointments of our lives. Gain for us too the grace to do His will with courage and untroubled hearts, so that we may radiate a joy and a gladness like yours in the service of Our Lord.

Prayer to follow St Thérèse of the Child Jesus

God our Father, you promised your kingdom to the little ones and the humble of heart. Give us the grace to walk confidently in the way of St Thérèse of the Child Jesus, so that helped by her prayers, we may see your glory and share in Your Kingdom.

In honour of St Thérèse of the Child Jesus of the Holy Face

Father in Heaven, you desire through St Thérèse of the Child Jesus and the Holy Face to remind the world of the merciful love that fills your heart, and the childlike trust we should have in you. We humbly thank you for crowning your ever-faithful child with such great glory, and for giving her wondrous power to bring to you, day by day, countless souls to praise you eternally.

St Thérèse of the Child Jesus and the Holy Face, remember your promise to do good upon earth; shower down your roses on those who invoke you, and obtain for us the graces we hope for from God's infinite goodness. (*Here mention your requests*)

Prayer for students

God our Father and creator, through the intercession of St Thérèse, we ask for insight and wisdom to see the signs of your love in the people and in the events of our lives. May we discern what we have to do as students and give us the strength to do it. Grant us success in our work and examinations.

Help us to believe in your great love for each one of us, so that we may live in truth and radiate your love in our lives. Through Christ our Lord. Amen.

A morning prayer of St Thérèse

O my God! I offer Thee all my actions of this day for the intentions and for the glory of the Sacred Heart of Jesus. I desire to sanctify every beat of my heart, my every thought, my simplest works, by uniting them to its infinite merits; and I wish to make reparation for my sins by casting them into the furnace of its merciful love.

O my God! I ask of Thee for myself and for those whom I hold dear, the grace to fulfill perfectly Thy Holy Will, to accept for love of Thee the joys and sorrows of this passing life, so that we may one day be united together in heaven for all Eternity. Amen.

Prayer of St Thérèse before the Tabernacle

Kneeling before the tabernacle, I can think of only one thing to say to our Lord; 'My God, you know that I love you.' And feeling that my prayer does not weary Jesus; knowing my weakness, he is satisfied with my good will.

When we grieve our incapacity to do good, our only resource is to offer the works of others. Herein lies the advantage of the Communion of Saints.

Prayer to the Holy Child

O little Jesus, my only treasure, I abandon myself to every one of thine adorable whims. I seek no other joy than that of making thee smile. Grant me the graces and the virtues of thy holy childhood, so that on the day of my birth into Heaven the angels and saints may recognise in thy little spouse… Thérèse of the Child Jesus.

Prayer to the Holy Face

O adorable Face of Jesus, sole beauty which ravisheth my heart, vouchsafe to impress on my soul thy divine likeness, so that it may not be possible for thee to look at thy spouse without beholding thyself. O my Beloved, for love of thee I am content not to see here on earth the sweetness of thy glance, nor to feel the ineffable kiss of thy sacred lips, but I beg of thee to inflame me with thy love, so that it may consume me quickly, and that soon Thérèse of the Holy Face may behold thy glorious countenance in Heaven.

Prayer for humility

I implore thee, dear Jesus, to send me a humiliation whensoever I try to set myself above others. Thou knowest my weakness. Each morning I resolve to be humble, and in the evening I recognise that I have often been guilty of pride. The sight of these faults tempts me to discouragement; yet I know that discouragement is itself but a form of pride. I wish therefore, O my God, to build all my trust upon thee. As thou canst do all things, deign to implant in my soul this virtue which I desire, and to obtain it from thy infinite mercy I will often say to thee: 'Jesus, meek and humble of heart, make my heart like unto thine.'

Act of oblation

O my God, O Most Blessed Trinity, I desire to love thee and to make thee loved - to labour for the glory of thy Church by saving souls here upon earth and by delivering those suffering in Purgatory. I desire to fulfil perfectly thy will, and to reach the degree of glory thou hast prepared for me in thy kingdom. In a word, I wish to be holy, but, knowing how helpless I am, I beseech thee, my God, to be thyself my holiness.

Since thou hast loved me so much as to give me thy Only-Begotten Son to be my Saviour and my Spouse, the infinite treasures of his merits are mine. I offer them gladly to thee, and I beg to thee to look on me through the eyes of Jesus, and in his Heart aflame with love. Moreover, I offer thee all the merits of the Saints in Heaven and on earth, together with their acts of love, and those of the holy Angels. Lastly, I offer thee, O Blessed Trinity, the love and the merits of the Blessed Virgin, my dearest Mother - to her I commit this oblation, praying her to present it to thee.

During the days of his life on earth her divine Son, my sweet Spouse, spoke these words: 'If you ask the Father anything in my Name, he will give it you.' Therefore I am certain thou wilt grant my prayer. O my God, I know that the more thou wishest to bestow, the more thou dost make us desire. In my heart I feel boundless desires, and I confidently beseech thee to take possession of my soul. I cannot receive thee in Holy Communion as often as I should wish; but art thou not all-powerful? Abide in me as thou dost in the tabernacle - never abandon thy little victim. I long to console thee for ungrateful sinners, and I implore thee to take from me all liberty to cause thee displeasure. If through weakness I should chance to fall, may a glance from thine eyes straightway cleanse my soul, and consume all my imperfections - as fire transforms all things into itself.

I thank thee, O my God, for all the graces thou hast granted me, especially for having purified me in the crucible of suffering. At the day of judgment I shall gaze with joy upon thee, carrying thy sceptre of the cross. And since thou hast deigned to give me this previous cross as my portion, I hope to be like unto thee in Paradise, and to behold the sacred wounds of thy Passion shine on my glorified body.

After earth's exile I hope to possess thee eternally, but I do not seek to lay up treasures in heaven. I wish to labour for thy love alone - with the sole aim of pleasing thee, of consoling thy Sacred Heart, and of saving souls who will love thee through eternity.

When the evening of life comes, I shall stand before thee with empty hands, because I do not ask thee, my God, to take account of my works. All our good deeds are blemished in thine eyes. I wish therefore to be robed with thine own justice, and to receive from thy love the everlasting gift of thyself. I desire no other throne but thee, O my Beloved!

In thy sight time is naught - 'one day is a thousand years'. Thou canst in a single instant prepare me to appear before thee.

In order that my life may be one act of perfect love, I offer myself as a holocaust to thy Merciful Love, imploring thee to consume me unceasingly and to allow the floods of infinite tenderness gathered up in thee to overflow into my soul, that so I may become a martyr of thy love, O my God! May this martyrdom one day release me from my earthly prison, after having prepared me to appear before thee, and may my soul take its flight - without delay - into the eternal embrace of thy merciful Love!

O my Beloved, I desire at every beat of my heart to renew this oblation an infinite number of times, 'till the shadows retire' and everlastingly I can tell thee my love face to face.

Where and how to venerate the Relics

On the following pages you will find details of when and where in England and Wales the Relics of St Thérèse will be visiting. Details of the venues' websites and phone numbers are given. It is possible that some details may have to be changed at the last minute.

In each venue the casket will be placed on display in a prominent place. There will be a Mass and other services each day, but most of the time will be left free for people to come and venerate the Relics and pray in whatever way they wish. Many of the venues will be open during the night as well.

Stewards will direct you in an orderly way to come and venerate the Relics. How you do that is entirely up to you: some people like to kiss the casket, or place their hands reverently upon it, while others may prefer just to pray quietly for a few moments. After you have been up to the Relics there may also be the opportunity, if space permits, for you to remain in the church and quietly pray and meditate.

Jesus said: "Seek first God's kingdom and his righteousness and all these other things shall be yours as well" (*Mt* 6:33). It is communion with God himself, and a holy way of living, that we seek above all as we come to venerate the Relics. For this reason, there will be plenty of priests available at each venue to hear your Confession or give spiritual advice.

But it is natural that many people will have specific intentions they also wish to bring, for a family member who is sick, for example, or for guidance to make the right decision about an important matter. As well as praying silently for these intentions, you will also be able to write them on a piece of paper and leave them with a steward for others to pray for. You can also e-mail them via the website: *www.catholicrelics.co.uk* - click on Contact or Send a Prayer.

Everyone is welcome to come and venerate the Relics. You don't have to be a practising Catholic or even a Christian to benefit from this unique opportunity. Just approach the Relics with as much openness as you can and with whatever faith you have. Wherever you are in life, this is an opportunity to take the next step on your journey towards God. If you are a practising Catholic, do not come alone! Invite someone else to come with you, especially those in any kind of need. Ask your parish priest if a coach or minibus can be organised from your parish to the nearest venue.

There will be a special welcome to those suffering from any illness or disability, and access will be made easy for them at every venue. In many places there will be a special service of healing for the sick.

Young people and children will also have a special part to play. In many cases there will be night vigils organised by young people. School parties are particularly welcome, and schools should contact their nearest venue to ensure ease of access.

Itinerary of the visit

Arrival date & time	Venue	Website and phone number	Departure date & time
Wednesday 16th September 11.00am	Portsmouth Cathedral Cathedral Church of St John the Evangelist Edinburgh Road Portsmouth PO1 3HG	*www.portsmouthcatholiccathedral.org.uk* Tel: 023 9282 6613	17th September 11.00am
Thursday 17th September 4.00pm	Plymouth Cathedral Cathedral Church of St Mary and St Boniface Wyndham Street Plymouth PL1 5HW	*www.plymouthcathedral.co.uk/index2.htm* Tel: 01752 662537	18th September 12 noon
Friday 18th September 3.00pm	St Teresa of Lisieux Eastwick Road Taunton Somerset TA2 7HF	Tel: 01823 333608	19th September 11.00am
Saturday 19th September 2.30pm	Birmingham Cathedral Metropolitan Cathedral Church of St Chad Cathedral House St Chad's Queensway B4 6EU	*www.stchadscathedral.org.uk* Tel: 0121 2362251	21st September 8.00am
Monday 21st September 8.30am	Sacred Heart and St Teresa 67 Coventry Road Coleshill Birmingham B46 3EA	Tel: 01675 463939	22nd September 11.00am
Tuesday 22nd September 3.30pm	Metropolitan Cathedral Church of St David 38 Charles Street Cardiff CF10 2SF	*www.cardiffmetropolitancathedral.org.uk* Tel: 029 2023407	23rd September 1.30pm

Arrival date & time	Venue	Website and phone number	Departure date & time
Wednesday 23rd September 3.00pm	St Teresa's 71 Gloucester Road North Filton Bristol BS34 7PL	Tel: 0117 9833938	24th September 10.00am
Thursday 24th September 3.00pm	Liverpool Cathedral Mount Pleasant Liverpool L3 5TQ	www.liverpoolmetro cathedral.org.uk Tel: 0151 7099222	25th September 3.00pm
Friday 25th September 4.30pm	Cathedral Church of St John the Evangelist Chapel Street Salford Manchester M3 5LL	Tel: 0161 8340333	27th September 7.30pm
Sunday 27th September 8.00pm	Manchester University Chaplaincy 335-9 Oxford Road Manchester M13 9PG	www.rc-chaplaincy-um.org.uk Tel: 0161 2731456	28th September 9.30am
Monday 28th September 4.00pm	Lancaster Cathedral Balmoral Road Lancaster LA1 3BT	www.lancastercathe dral.org.uk Tel: 01524 384820	30th September 11.00am
Wednesday 30th September 3.00pm	St Andrew's Worswick Street Newcastle upon Tyne NE1 6UW	Tel: 0191 2321892	1st October 10.30am
Thursday 1st October 6.00pm	York Minster Church House Ogleforth York YO1 7JN	www.yorkminster.org Tel: 01904 557200	2nd October 12.00 noon

Arrival date & time	Venue	Website and phone number	Departure date & time
Friday 2nd October 2.00pm	Middlesbrough Cathedral Dalby Way Coulby Newham Middlesbrough TS8 0TW	www.middlesbrough rccathedral.org Tel: 01642 597750	3rd October 12.00 noon
Saturday 3rd October 2.00pm	Leeds Cathedral Great George Street Leeds LS2 8BE	www.leedscathedral. org.uk Tel: 0113 2454545	5th October 10.30am
Monday 5th October 5.00pm	Nottingham Cathedral Derby Road Nottingham NG1 5AE	www.stbarnabasnotti ngham.org.uk Tel: 0115 9539839	6th October 12.00 noon
Tuesday 6th October 3.30pm	National Shrine of Our Lady of Walsingham Slipper Chapel Houghton St Giles NR22 6AL	www.walsingham.org .uk Tel: 01328 820217	7th October 1.30pm
Wednesday 7th October 6.00pm	Oxford Oratory 25 Woodstock Road Oxford OX2 6HA	www.oxfordoratory. org.uk Tel: 01865 315800	8th October 4.30pm
Thursday 8th October 6.00pm	St Joseph's Austenwood Common Chalfont St Peter Gerrards Cross Bucks. SL9 8RY	www.carmelite.org.uk /Gcross.html Tel: 01753 886581	9th October 11.00am
Friday 9th October 2.00pm	Aylesford Priory Aylesford ME20 7BX	www.thefriars.org.uk Tel: 01622 717272	11th October 5.00pm

Arrival date & time	Venue	Website and phone number	Departure date & time
Sunday 11th October 7.30pm	Carmelite Church Our Lady of Mt Carmel and St Simon Stock 41 Kensington Church Street Kensington W8 4BB	*www.carmelitechurch.org* Tel: 020 7937 9866	12th October 7.30am
Monday 12th October 7.00pm	Westminster Cathedral Ambrosden Avenue London SW1P 1QH	*www.westminstercathedral.org.uk* Tel: 020 7798 9055	15th October 4.30pm

Further information

http://www.catholicrelics.co.uk - The official website of the visit to England and Wales.

http://www.thérèseoflisieux.org - Without question this is the best website about St Thérèse. Well-organised and attractively presented, it contains a huge amount of information about every aspect of St Thérèse's life and mission.

http://thérèse-de-lisieux.cef.fr/ang/frameang.htm - The official site (in English) of the sanctuary in Lisieux, including some good photos.

http://www.ewtn.com/thérèse/thérèse.htm - Eternal Word Television has lots about the spirituality and message of St Thérèse.

http://www.littleflower.org/learn/littleflower.asp - Website of the Little Flower Society.

http://www.carmelite.com/thérèse2002/vonbal.htm - The great theologian Hans Urs von Balthasar writes about the Little Way of Spiritual Childhood.

http://www.ronrolheiser.com/pdfs/perennial.pdf - Fr Ronald Rolheiser on the perennial fascination of St Thérèse.

http://www.catholictradition.org/lisieux/lisieux.htm - A traditionalist site with an excellent collection of photos.

http://www.stthérèse.com - Site of the Irish national office of St Thérèse.

http://www.ocd.pcn.net/OC-OCD/OC-OCD3EN.htm - The Letter of the Carmelite Superiors General on the occasion of the declaration of St Thérèse as a Doctor of the Church.

Endnotes

[1] This statement is expanded on by the *Directory on Popular Piety and the Liturgy* issued by the Congregation for Divine Worship late in 2001: "The term 'relics of the saints' principally signifies the bodies - or notable parts of the bodies - of the saints who, as distinguished members of Christs's mystical body and as temples of the Holy Spirit in virtue of their heroic sanctity, now dwell in heaven, but who once lived on earth. Objects which belonged to the saints, such as personal objects, clothes and manuscripts are also considered relics, as are objects which have touched their bodies or tombs such as oils, cloths and images" (CTS 2002, Do 682, §236). This really just summarizes the longer statement, to which is refers, of the Council of Trent (Session XXV): "The holy Synod enjoins on all bishops, and others who sustain the office and charge of teaching, that, agreeably to the usage of the Catholic and Apostolic Church, received from the primitive times of the Christian religion, and agreeably to the consent of the holy Fathers, and to the decrees of sacred Councils, they especially instruct the faithful diligently concerning the intercession and invocation of saints; the honour (paid) to relics; and the legitimate use of images: teaching them, that the saints, who reign together with Christ, offer up their own prayers to God for men; that it is good and useful suppliantly to invoke them, and to have recourse to their prayers, aid, (and) help for obtaining benefits from God, through His Son, Jesus Christ our Lord, who is our alone Redeemer and Saviour ... Also, that the holy bodies of holy martyrs, and of others now living with Christ - which bodies were the living members of Christ, and the temple of the Holy Ghost, and which are by Him to be raised unto eternal life, and to be glorified - are to be venerated by the faithful; through which (bodies) many benefits are bestowed by God on men."

[2] See 1 Corinthians 6.12-20. noon

[3] Already in the New Testament we find that handkerchiefs and other garments which had touched the flesh of St Paul at Ephesus cured diseases (see *Ac* 19:12).

[4] Relics of the second century martyr St Polycarp were described as "more valuable than precious stones and finer than refined gold"